Lucid Life

A Collection of Lyrical Poetry

Catherine R. Berra

Lucid Life: A Collection of Lyrical Poetry
Published by Sassypants Press
Denver, CO

ISBN: 978-1-7342063-0-2

Poetry

Cover art by Alexander Aziz
Author photo by Jennifer Risdon

QUANTITY PURCHASES: Schools, companies, professional groups, clubs, and other organizations may qualify for special terms when ordering quantities of this title. For information, email Sassypantspress@comcast.net.

This book is printed in the United States of America.

SASSYPANTS PRESS

For my son, Alexander,
who at his birth,
gave me life.

Contents

Birth 1

Life 13

Love 31

Loss...55

Journey...69

Poet's Prayer

Writer writes and pen flows to page
Give me strength to hear such change
Lift me up, my eyes will see
The amazing gift freely given to me.

Write your voice on pages white
And give of yourself by expressing sight
Do not fear rejection deep
For your gift is for giving
And not to keep.

Birth

My Son

Little boy
with his mother's eyes,
learn to be simple, gentle and wise.

Little boy
with an old soul's mind,
learn to be giving, generous and kind.

Little man,
my life's greatest gift,
learn to love, for life is swift.

Little man,
you are precious to me,
and the world holds treasure for you to see.

I will take you
as far as I can
and when you are ready,
I'll let go of your hand.
I'll watch from a distance
but always be near
Proudly I'll help you
calm all your fears.

And guide you along
as life's struggles come
and bathe in the sunshine
that you shall become.

Love is a feeling
I learned when you came
my son,
the whole world will know you by name.

Free

Beyond the strength
That this daily life takes me
Into the light
The morning sky wakes me.

Each day as before
Each task a great chore
Give me courage to get through the day.

So far as my good heart and soul will allow me
My child will get love
As his needs they surround me.

My mind fills with desire
My heart is on fire
For something I haven't yet found.

Out there my creativeness
Will move me farther
Yet now I must try to be a great mother.

Each day something new
My son, pure and true
My life has been blessed
And I'm free.

Climb

Young man stands
On steps I build
Strong am I
To climb that hill
First before him
Pave the way
Ensure such safety
The steps I've laid.

Climb now higher
His strides they come
Right behind me
Almost run
Soon he'll pass me
Reach the top
And stand above
Then make a stop
And wave goodbye
Then choose his course
As I look upon him
My smile forced.
Away now boy
Be gone be free
Adventure out
The world to see
And when you're ready
Continue, climb
Build more steps
On top of mine.

Make them sturdy
Make them strong
So your children climb
And sing your song.

Truly His

Like shifting clouds
and moving earth,

This time enlightens
all my worth.

And stands me on
the quiet shore,

In hopes that I
shall journey forth.

And find another
righteous cause,

To steer my heart
and see what was.

For now the was
becomes the is,

And the life I gave,
is truly his.

Where I Walk

Where I walk
Depends solely on the destiny of my heart

Where I rest
Surely navigates my dreams

When I weep
My soul releases pain

But then I turn and walk again

Where I move
Depends on the balance in my mind
Treading toward illustrious intentions
Sometimes fulfilled.

Where we're going, my son and I
God truly marked for guidance

Though lost in thought and considering your future
The thrill of life never ceases
Never calms
Nor shall your thirst for more and more

Where I walk
I step most lightly
Daring to step aside

Soon you shall fly in your own right
Soaring, my child, in flight so gracious

Live this life
As only once
For where you walk
Yours, too, shall follow.

Life

True Beauty

What is God's true beauty
And what in life is grand
Is it a red rose petal
Or a soft, sweet baby's hand?

And what will last forever
And what shall pass unseen
Do we live life missing
What there could have been?

What are life's real treasures
Do we live our lives in vain
Seeking out the unimportant
Only to seek again?

Right before our very eyes
The truth will be revealed
If only our eyes focus clearly
On what we truly feel.

Your heart reveals true kindness
Your words express the truth
Unconditional, caring love
Is what I have learned from you.

Because you see the sunshine
Through the dark and shifting clouds
You remind me that the glory
Is in front of me right now.

What is God's true beauty
And what in life is true?
It is a woman with a heart of gold
So simply
It is you.

Save Me

My protection it has failed me
Stabbed my heart
Impaled me

What I covered scared me
Afraid of life
So take me

Change me
Make me whole
Release the pain
Release my soul

The loss of you
Has changed me
Tears have cleansed
And drained me.

I see now
The safety
Of errant fear
So plainly

Dreams are meant to save me
From pain so great it frames me.

I loved you
Oh so plainly
Sorrow kept
Insanely

Weep and mourn
Now daily
Calm my breath
And take me

I reach for you
Go saintly
Goodbye my love
You saved me

…and the little girl, she disappeared, she walked away with all my fears.

Have

What I can't have
Is right in front of me
Blinding me
Moving me

What I can't see
Is clear and plain to me
And I'll be free

But what I can't stop
Is what has gone before
Wanting more
Open door

And there he was indeed
Like magnetic pull
Heart so full
Pull the wool

Then I saw her face
Looking up at him
Her daddy's grin
Can't have this again

What lesson now is there to learn?
What I can't have
What I can't be
This game, it does not set me free.

Open Cage

Irony meet me
Your walls do not defeat me
Surround these certain days
Yet leave me in my open cage

Protecting my small life
Until the time is right
Until he's on his own
And I am sure he's flown

Irony consume me
Best intentions doom me
Attempting what is right
Prolongs this lonely fight

Open cage so sturdy
I'm proud and oh so worthy
Goodness lights my way
Small steps most every day.

Undone

She paused to rest, her burdens full
Her mind it tired, the push, the pull.
She tried to breathe, to catch some air
But found her breath, it was not there.

The journey made thus far was fine
The plans, the goals, the gift of time.
But where, she wondered, had she gone?
The she once known, the she undone.

Now moving forward, she takes small strides
Because her path has changed inside.
Conflicted dreams and passions died
How, she wonders, do you restart life?

She ponders options and moves along
As her daughters start to sing their songs.
What will be will soon become
Tomorrow's journey, toward which she'll run.

Shine

In the scheme of all the living
blessed by a strength of will,
the legacy that you've created
now stands to be fulfilled.

From little grew abundance,
from hardship came belief,
that forward moving progress
would not happen in your sleep.

Yet to rise above beginnings
means nothing without proof,
that getting begets giving
and that honor thrives with truth.

Lucky are those with nothing
for they have only hope to rise,
you lend a hand to lift them
and shine light into their eyes.

The cost of having plenty
with giving, does atone
and reminds us through your adage
that no one succeeds alone.

Beginnings
and Endings

Each day I close my weary eyes
The end of hours passed and tried
Open them whence day appears
Continue this for years and years.

Each breath I take it starts as deep
Exhaled unconscious yet consciously free
Another comes with no thought or care
A beginning, too, with sweet ending air.

And as life continues the beginnings fuse
With endings always like a faithful muse
No worries kept or frets to fail
The beginnings are the ending's tale.

I watch the day as it comes and goes
I watch the too short life of the rose
I see you come to fill my days
Then vanish, ending what once was safe.

I feel the pain of your departure most
For the beginning was what I treasured so
Now beginning is my task again
And your ending began this exhausting plan.

Yet to begin again sans an ending sure
Delays the courage, avoids the lure
The heart beats surely once proved to mend
And I turn to begin what I know shall soon end.

Up

Little, pleasant point of view
Created, paused for interlude
Thwarted thoughts of pain and sorrow
Put aside to admit tomorrow

Telling, poignant shapes of light
Escape my lids and seem so bright
Lay me here in sadness still
Force the life into my will

Bitter, sweet and hurtful man
Reject me now and make your stand
Force me forward into the fear
I will survive but hold you dear

Broken, healing is my heart
With time and absence, I shall start
Take the blindfold from my eyes
Its time I looked toward the skies.

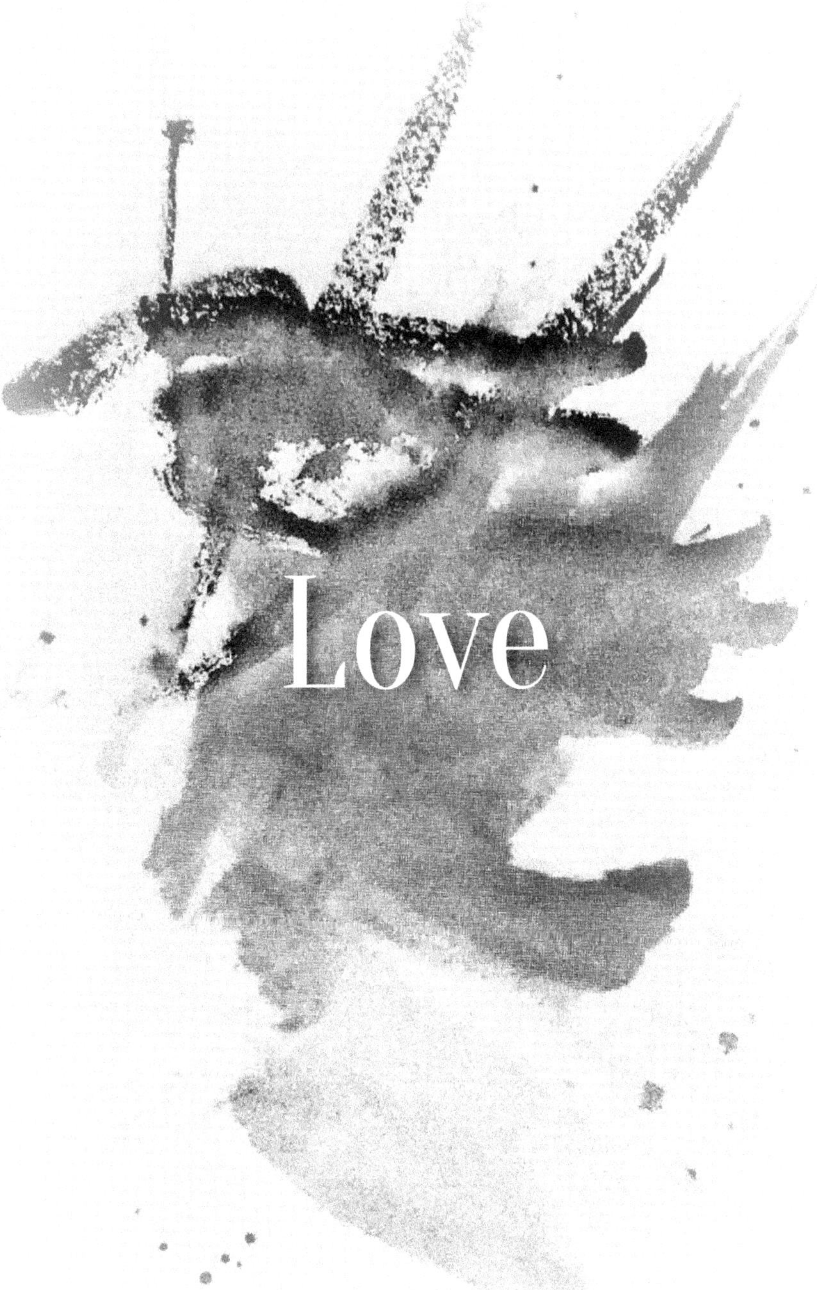

Love

Significance

The significance
Of what I would say to you
Would in no way ever
Crystallize the passion a dream contains
Nor could a dream ever
Truthfully force the outcome
Of my never-ending desire for you
For all passion settles
Just as fierce winds eventually lighten
Just as the clouds inevitably
Dissipate for the sun to shine.

So I am waiting for my heart
To cease yearning
Waiting for the color of your eyes
Fearing
That the strongest craving
Some day dies.

Song

There was a song I should have sung
You'd given me such voice
Oh how the fates altered my plan
No, I had not a choice.

The time I'd sing would lift me up
Beyond my lonely time
And now I sing, avert my eyes
Toward the bluest skies.

Do you reside so far from me
That songs cannot be heard?
Do you hear the loving tune
I sing with silent words?

Shall I sing now that you've gone
For whom, sweet melody?
The voice I'd saved for your sweet ears
Was to be our symphony.

Such silence drives my heart to break
For I wish to sing this song
For you, my love, now silent, too
I'd waited far too long.

There is a song I'll try to sing
If I am blessed again
With someone as you were, my love
Yet, I do not know just when.

So look upon me, throw some stars
Remind me of your light
As I recall you every day
My eyes are clear and bright.

Facet

Cautioned heart and excited mind
What is this facet that I find?

A part of something grand and large
Or reminder's cue that heart's in charge?

The bluest eyes and wanting stare
A friend I knew, I feel, somewhere.

And let the time with ease reveal
The quiet voice time cannot steal.

The voice that calls, the voice that seeks
To find the ears to hear such piece.

My cautioned heart has found the strength
To chance this time, to go this length.
To falter yet continue still
To give my love, his life to fill?
And kindness does indeed remain
The gesture sweet, the kiss not plain.

What does this life mean after all?
That love is wondrous, and worries small?
That pain subsides, I have loved before
That caution is
Life's search for more.

Plea

Against my heart's unrelenting plea
I released the love that conquered me
For reasons cruel and reasons sweet
We said goodbye, yet now I weep

To have your hand so strong and true
Be forced again to abandon you
This life is short, unkind and strange
Oh how my heart resists this change

My tired mind diminished much
A simple kiss, my loving touch
I know I was away in mind
Now rested, crave your love so kind

Forever lost the gift of you?
Has time caused pain to stifle truth?
The path we walked, that path once grand
Shall I walk alone
Or may I take your hand?

So desperate was my fearful soul
Afraid of things that crept in cold
My son had turned a corner black
And left me helpless, speechless, sad

You watched and reached and I pushed away
You did not deserve his hate's display
So sorry for this sadness caused
Your strength I see now gives me pause

Forgive me please for weakness shown
For lack of strength and a peaceful home
I know not ways to battle hate
And what you endured causes constant shame

Your happiness is all I wish
Perchance with me, or have I missed
The time unfair and your weary heart
Is it too late for a lover's start?

Muse

And so the days have tempted truth
Its course so surely diverts this muse.
Where hope and smiles once filled the page
Replaced unfairly by unfair age.

Go now beauty, fly now pain
Force the heart to withstand this shame.
Fear not time and fear not death
For love exists in every breath.

And as it leaves us so does it come
For love begets love, is not undone.
So thank the winds that caused same paths
And bid goodbye as the fork is mapped.

Diverted now with different dreams
New paths will bring you home for free.
And hold on tightly to all things shared
And gently release that breath of air.

For on my lips are words of depth
Such words so honest as I wept.
Close your eyes and see my smile
I'll see yours as well, my sweet man-child.

Brave Silence

A brave silence today
Force my heart closed
And my words kept at bay

A cause meant to instill
The facts, oh, so brutal
Shall not break your will

You move on with closed heart
Hoping my memory
Will soon seem so far

And I try to be free
Of what could have been
If we felt differently

Yet the day now is gone
Passed with deep breaths
Waiting calm for the dawn

Where do you sleep tonight?
Caught up in caution
Or through with the fight?

My heart tires of this
Hanging by thread
That would break with your kiss.

Carry You

What do I want to learn that's new?

I want to learn how to carry you.

In my hands and in my heart

I'll make this learning a magnificent art.

I'll study all the shallow depths

And ask to hear your secrets kept.

A student of your very being

I'd work so hard and hone the seeing.

Learn the lessons to love you right

And hope it's what I've longed to find.

I Want to Be

I want to be your loving muse
And dance until you smile
Keep the sorrows hidden deep
Forgotten for a while.

I'll come and go as conjured forth
Your pleasure for a kiss
Delight and hold your darkest hours
And replace them all with bliss.

Connected by the universe
Yet far away in form
I send small messages of love
To keep your heart so warm.

The reason is a mystery
God's plan for me a test
Why I'm sent to honor you
Confuses but seems best.

So let me sing a song for you
Or touch your skin to calm
This is a journey and you a path
That I must travel on.

I want to be your loving muse
To care for you to sleep
You know I'm here, just call my name
Eternity will keep.

Purpose

What purpose have you come for
The lesson in your smile
Shine so bright
Then fade away
Along the trodden miles.

A weary heart it hopes for
Connection and relief
Offer light
Then fade to black
Typical retreat?

The purpose as I see it
A lesson I must learn
Come and stay
A price I'd pay
Waiting for my turn.

Heavenly

The fates, they played an unfair hand
Caught me off guard with the sweetest man
Forced my movement toward his light
This blinding thing is far too bright

His spirit, who has pulled me in?
How did this manifest and when?
A pull so strong I had to go
To kiss his mouth, to somehow know

And leave me wondering if his spirit craves
Something from me I already gave
A random meeting by two similar souls
On a frigid day, found warmth imposed

I wonder still if I've been fooled
For the fates can make or break the rules
For now, I'll smile and see him kind
And avoid the thoughts that fill my mind

In life, so short, why question chance?
Why bother denying another dance?
The soul searches on until this is done
He's come along, and brought the sun.

Wild Pony

My daughter,
said her father once,
is like a wild pony.
Her spirit is so strong and fierce
I fear she might get lonely.

What man could ever rein her in
and hold her spirit still?
My daughter, she is absolute
in beauty and in will.

Her loyalty is like no other
her creativeness unique.
That crazy, wild, pony spirit
must be what the right man seeks.

My daughter,
said her father once,
is hard to hold and handle.
The man that wins her heart and soul
must also hold a candle.

To light her way when she can't see
to remind her not to run,
to offer a gentle, patient hand
so she doesn't come undone.

Her spirit shines and blinds the weak
her wild ways they test.
My wish is that she'll find that man
to tame her soul
and let her rest.

Loss

Light

Your skin to touch
How I did crave
Now lays beneath your final grave.

Your lips to kiss
So seldom done
Now on a hill and in the sun.

Your hands I held
While you were dying
You lay asleep while I mourned, crying.

Your eyes to see
You must have known
My heart's true fondness, my love had grown.

Now I grieve you
Lost chance I kept
And love you forever, curse your final sleep.

Oh, pain and sorrow
Oh, passion fire
Oh, dreams and yearning
Unrequited desire.

The day, it begins
Move forward, anew
Why must I dim the light that was you?

I curse my intentions
I curse what I craved
I curse what was taken forever away.

And God did he dangle
Such beauty and faith
I believe nothing shall soon take its place.

How shall I breathe
With my tears, falling?
How shall I dream, I reach for you, calling.

I lay on my pillow at night feeling small
And wait once again as the tears, they do fall.

Numb

I close my eyes and think of you
Your body heavy in the darkened room
I let my mind go blank and free
Block out the light that is blinding me.

Those thoughts of what we could have been
Now smothered until it reaches end
And then I turn and pretend to sleep
While he holds me close, I silently weep.

The tears don't fall because I am strong
I'll not give in; I know you're wrong
And yet I lay here empty and numb
With my lover's kiss, I pretend to succumb.

How many days will my heart be bound
To the memory of the love I had found
And let it slip from my fingers fast
How many days until it's past?

And in the dark my eyes do search
For the glory and prayer of an empty church
For I play a part now numb and surreal
To bid my time for my heart to heal.

Down

I pray the light shines upon you
On the path you choose to take
I pray that friends surround you
As you make your way.

Remember hills and valleys
Remember all you've seen
Remember that I love you
And share all that I've been.

No, I am most imperfect
In human shape and form
My tragedies are personal
And teeter on the norm.

But oh, sometimes the pain comes
It ravages my heart
And this time was the very worst
This time, my breath cut short.

Yes, I did so love him
In my quiet, distant way
For my history has been to look
But never take away.

Down as far as I can be
My soul it craves the light
For I am afraid I've sunk below
Where I ever thought I might.

Help me please to stand up tall
And smile and laugh again
It will come, I'm sure in time
But now it feels the end.

Loss of Dreams

The loss of dreams and previous perception
Evolves my life toward inevitable redemption.
What once was vital
What once was true
With a few cruel words
Revealed all of you.

I stepped toward the darkness
And chanced true rejection
Knowing all the while
It was my own reflection.

For what came before
I'd hidden too long
Confronting all the darkness
Created this sweet song.

And I'll be fine
And I'll be free
Because I'm the one who was repressing me.

The past has crept in silent steps
And appeared unflawed
To erase my regret.

Turn Corners

You stand down the hill
To wide open space
You see in the distance
The vastness, the grace

You look to the skies
For his breath in the breeze
And wonder aloud
And ask if he sees.

All the beauty he's given
The wonder he's blessed
The stars by the millions
He's hung to impress.

The grass it grows greener
The icy creek thaws
But the passage of time
Leaves your heart no less raw.

But the gift of this place
Must be magic, it feels
As you step into the garden
Let the mud cake your heels.

What sorrow, so broken
So far away, cries
You wait patiently, hoping
For those big butterflies.

Turn corners, grow wiser
As life hands us fate
Stand up, keep on moving
Come on in, close the gate.

And your brother did love you
So precious his ways
His memory lives quietly
And enhances today.

Lucid

I cannot breathe
I see no light
I'm drowning in
The lucid fight
So clear, yet dark
And far away
Oh, blessed truth
Don't end this day.

Such sorrow still
Such stifled time
To break so free
From fate sublime
Nor take what breath
Such life would birth
Such glory moved
Upon my earth.

I say a prayer
For answers kind
For eyes to see
Where I've been blind
For hand to hold
For help to be
What comes from where
My heart is free.

Oh, take my hand
And move it, flow
So words become
The words I know.

Journey

The Struggle

The Struggle steers a vivid pause
it cast away the artist's cause.

So natural once with pen in hand
this fight from past cruel intentions hands
this artist such a long reprise
and yet with time opens different eyes
the Struggle came with fluid force
yet time now reveals a different course.

This distinct new path appears in sight,
in the distance lies the artist's light.
The final length, the uphill climb
this artist's strength gained over time.
With cautious steps she makes her way
to revive her gift and cast away
that struggle once a burden large
in layers shed to heal her heart.

Path

A vast and varied question plays
Inside my pondering soul
Of truth, of fairness justly proved
To complete me, make me whole.

Until a righteous path I find
Or learn to seek direction
No, peace will never enter here
Its cure that of perfection.

So play along and dream in sleep
True goodness waits to give
A chance that I've been searching for
In order to simply live.

Unsettled Soul

My heart still travels
So many miles
Goes nowhere then turns
And reflects for a while.

Uncertain direction
Everywhere my heart goes
Until I find peace
An unsettled soul.

Until there is calmness
Until I really know
Until you come with me
An unsettled soul.

Far in the distance
Your eyes shine so bright
Here, I think of you
To hold you in the night.

But I'll settle for growing
For learning, then I'll know
God help teach me patience
With my unsettled soul.

Help me believe
There will come my time
For direction and sureness
After all of these miles.

So I travel this distance
And I travel alone
God please teach me patience
I'm an unsettled soul.

Unsung Rhyme

Incidentally, things stand still
Our minds bear witness
To unsolved thrills
We lend our ear
And lend our time
All but for the unsung rhyme.

Coincidentally, we are here
Making way for
Distant years.
Cause, effect
And fate and life
What we've seen
Shall pass sans strife.

Hold this thought
Inside so deep
For when you're gone
No one to keep.

Find

The day will come when I shall find
The answers to questions plaguing my mind

The clouds will lift, the sky reflect
All of the pain I've tried to perfect

Here and now I am not content
Restless and mindful my heart's intent

Carry on for the sake of despair
So as not to alter the heart in repair

Do not disturb the path I must seek
Where will I find it, my weary small feet

How many mountains do we climb before
The summit we've reached will open a door

When will the desire to continue this die?
When will the tears be gone from my eyes?

I pray on my knees for strength and for peace
By my son I'm inspired and shall never cease

Lift me up and reveal a sign
For the sake of my heart
As it tires
So do I.

Prayer in
the Woods,
My Church

The birds are the chorus
Oh, how they adore us
As we make our way through the woods

The catbird reminds us
That time is behind us
And the trail up ahead is still good

My feet, they meander
And my mind, it still wanders
As I think of you every day

The leaves how they flutter
Not a word do I mutter
As I silence my mind and I pray.

Murmuration

The ebbing and the flowing
The coming and the going
The inning and the outing
The screaming and the shouting

The loving and the hating
The getting and the waiting
The living and the dying
The laughing and the crying

The moving and the staying
The hiding and displaying
The sleeping and the waking
The destroying and the making

The love I have is ready
The hand I have is steady
I wait for kind elation
I fly, sweet murmuration.

Beauty

I came upon such Beauty and light
An animal spirit to mirror my life
A teacher of patience, of presence and change
This Beauty was gifted to me for my pain.

To exit the entrance I kept going through
Hoping to find something different and new.
And exiting finally to a new altered course
Shown to me simply by a magnificent horse.

She came strong and willing, to journey together
From there we find trust and a bond beyond measure.

Where we are going and where we shall ride
Is just Beauty and fate
with God's grace by our side.

Other Side of the World – Alaska

Dip my fingers into the water
Temperate smoothness, big surprise
Eagles are soaring, this life is not boring
Fill my wonderous eyes.

Far away searching for something
On the other side of the world
The vastness and quiet
The calm and the wild
The remoteness makes me unsure.

But the eagles have been here forever
And they fly on their course as they do
No matter if life's floating smoothly
Or we're searching our hearts through and through.

The other side of the world gave me calm
Light rain cleared the dust from my brain
Smooth waters took me away for a while
To adjust how I've managed the pain.

And coming home was a blessing
For that peace and remoteness remains
In my heart, in my mind as reminder
That the choice to be peaceful sustains.

Constant

A constant moving fluid life
your words have kept me sane,
a friend since way before this age
whose goodness still remains.

We teach each other carelessly
our different lives converge,
as time it passes quickly still
and interweaves what's learned.

So far, so good, so let us go
the place we are is here,
not there or any other space
those little girls endear.

The constant strength you tend to give
without knowing all it means,
lifelong friendship, a gift and light
easing pain and all, it seems.

Thank you, friend for being there
both near and far in places,
the time we have together reveals
those smiling little girl faces.

And on we go as time it flies
the phases ebb and flow,
what we've become as separate girls
is all that we have known.

And all that we have known is truth
the ups and downs, the stages,
our friendship is a constant light
one that transcends our ages.

So, smile my friend and feel my thanks
your goodness helps me through.
I hope my hand has been held out
and bestowed the same upon you.

Prove

She's got to do what she's got to do
Avoid the truth to make it through
Adjust the light to hide the scars
From all of her internal wars.

Sneak right past the scary door
The one she'd be better turning for
The day will come when she'll take those breaths
And move toward the path that's best.

For now she verges on that move
Fearing what she'll need to prove
Knowing that it doesn't matter
What others think, or how they flatter.

Years have passed in this righteous cage
Now she sees that she's been brave
Just needing something to hold on tight
To release the grip and enhance her flight.

Late Bloomer

It takes time to find the shadow
The dark remains behind
Turning fast to see it
Is like a toy shop wind.

Round and round for nothing
The sun it casts your truth
Behind you is the sunshine
That illuminates just you.

Now walk ahead determined
Keep facing toward that view
The length of time it takes to feel
The lateness of your bloom.

For time it has one purpose
To move our days toward end
Just remember keep end in sight
Because sunshine is your friend.

Older, Wiser

Older, wiser, bolder, wider
Not many things that haven't tried her.

Bitter, colder, they should've told her
Life goes on and trust, it molds her.

Coming through the years of lessons
Tired, wired, released possessions.

Simplify and lose the meaning
In all the stuff and all the gleaning.

Quiet, solemn, lovely, true
Age takes ahold and softens you.

Resigned, resolved, wrinkled smile
Grateful, giddy for all the miles.

Future, limits, questions, love
The answers she's been thinking of.

Manly, shelter, peaceful, true
She dreams of living a life with you.

Writing, feeling, knowing, home
These virtues she carries, but not alone.

Day

On a happy day
The seagulls sway
Children play
And daylight fades
Too quickly

On a happy day
You go your way
Hear what they say
And let the rain
Fall gently.

What Else

What else but
Love, loss and time
What else but the sweet sublime
Paths that lead to sudden change
Forced upon us, bitter, strange

Courses failed and courses tried
Taken from us, almost pried
Chosen quest so sudden, halted
Choices made and dreams so faulted

Part my waters, give me leave
To move so swiftly, let me breathe
What else but
Truth, heart and soul

What else but
The journey's toll
Subtle chance and perfect plans
A flight, a flutter from our hands

Fate so wicked, fate so kind
Given us as faltered signs
And must we worry, must we wane
To chance a broken heart again?
To risk the rapture
Risk the joy
Plant the seed
For our heart's employ?

Dare not seek for it shall appear
When blindness calls you
Tempers fear
Lest you seek to fill voids vast
Time will teach you
Surrender past.

About the Author

Catherine Berra is an avid writer, poet, horsewoman, and world traveler, a dedicated mother and friend, and a lover of nature. She holds a BA in communications/business management from Metropolitan State University in Denver and an Animals and Human Health certification from the University of Denver. For more than twenty years, her career in Washington, D.C., revolved around senior-level logistical and management support to a U.S. ambassador and technical writing at the State Department. Upon her return to Colorado in 2014, she resumed her passion for writing and giving back to the world. She is the founder of BeHerd, LLC, an equine-assisted, confidence-building activities program. Catherine resides in Littleton, Colorado, is the proud mother of Alexander Aziz, and relishes her role as caretaker of her rescue horse, Dancer. You can find her at sassypantspress@comcast.net.

www.ingramcontent.com/pod-product-compliance
Lightning Source LLC
Chambersburg PA
CBHW032013040426
42448CB00006B/613